POPULAR
SCIENCE®
KIDS

Weird Wild AND Wonderful

275 Amazing Animals From Tiny to Tall, Furry to Feathered, Creepy to Cute

CENTENNIAL BOOKS

A puffin's beak changes color during the year. It's brightest during the spring months, when it matches its orange feet!

POPULAR
SCIENCE®

KIDS

Weird
Wild
AND
Wonderful

275 Amazing Animals From Tiny to Tall, Furry to Feathered, Creepy to Cute

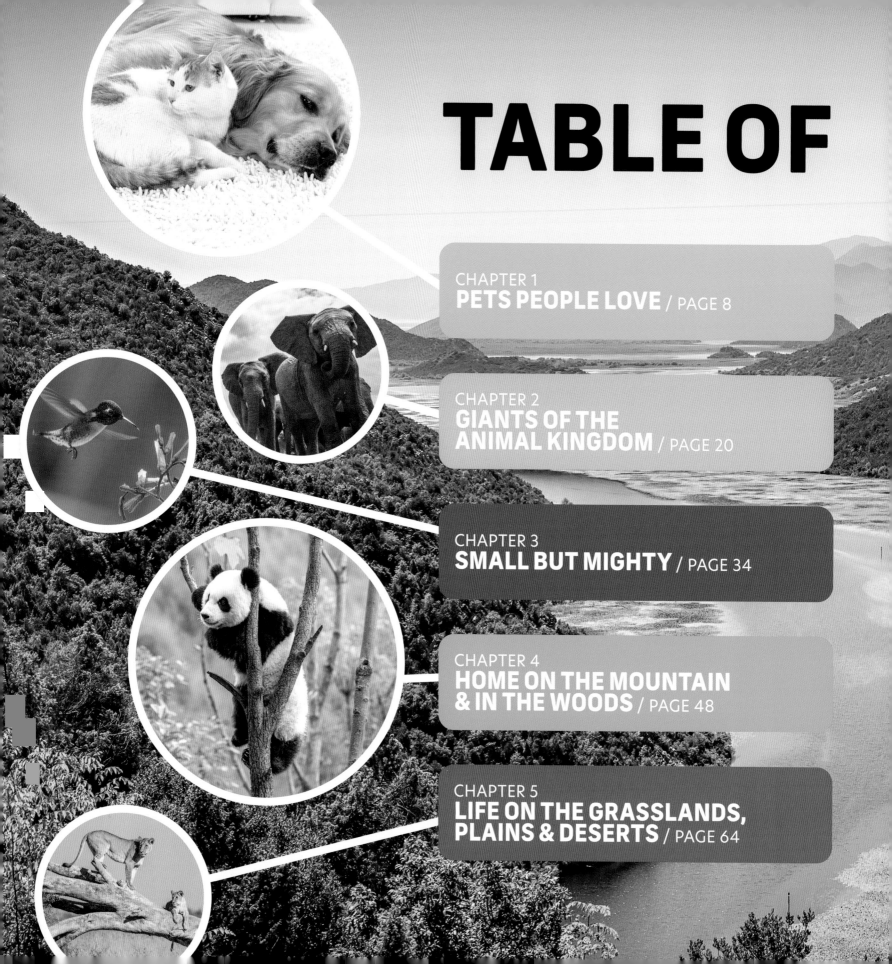

TABLE OF

CONTENTS

A PLANET FULL OF

Here's a guessing game for you. How many kinds, or species, of animals live on Earth? How many roam across lands near and far? How many bugs and other creepy-crawly things hide away underground? And how many make their lives in the different waters of the world?

Would you say hundreds of species live among us? Thousands? Even millions or trillions?

If you're not sure, you're not alone. Even scientists play this guessing game. That's because new species are being discovered all the time. And some species, sadly, are dying out.

VERTEBRATES
Animals That Have a Backbone

Warm-Blooded

Cold-Blooded

MAMMALS	BIRDS	FISH	REPTILES	AMPHIBIANS	INSECTS
• Have hair or fur • Feed their babies their own milk • Give birth to live young	• Have wings, feathers and bills • Lay eggs • Have a special skeleton	• Live in water • Breathe with gills • Have fins • Most have scales	• Are covered with scales • Lay eggs or bear live young • Have lungs	• Breathe through their skin • Change shape as they grow up	• Have a shell • Have antennae • Contain a head, thorax and abdomen

Bat, Eagle, Fox, Owl, Dolphin, Tiger, Ostrich — Salmon, Goldfish, Angelfish, Seahorse — Tortoise, Chameleon, Snake, Crocodile — Frog, Toad, Newt — Earwig, Ant, Butterfly, Bee

ANIMALS!

From spiders to seahorses, so many amazing creatures live in our world!

So what's the big number? Some scientists believe there are close to 9 million different animal species—maybe more! Most of those millions haven't even been discovered yet, and finding those species might take a while. But right here you can discover a whole world of weird, wild and wonderful creatures we do know about.

Animals are divided into two main groups: Vertebrates (VUHR-tuh-brayts) have a backbone, or spine—like us (and apes, fish, birds and reptiles). Invertebrates (in-VUHR-tuh-brayts) do not have a spine, such as insects, worms, crabs and many more species. Here's a look at how scientists sort different types of animals.

INVERTEBRATES
Animals That Don't Have a Backbone

ARACHNIDS	MOLLUSKS	ANNELIDS	CRUSTACEANS	ECHINODERMS	PROTOZOA
• Have eight legs • Bodies are in two sections • Lay eggs • Have a shell	• Have soft bodies • Use a muscular foot but no legs • Some have a shell	• Have a long, segmented body • Have a hollow body cavity • Many live in soil	• Have a hard, protective shell • Often have antennae • Mostly in water	• Live in water • Have spines on their skins/ • No external skeleton	• Tiny, single-celled animals • Most can only be seen with a microscope

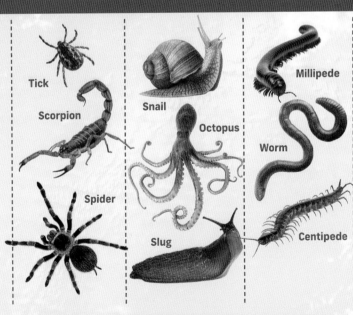

Tick

Scorpion

Spider

Snail

Octopus

Slug

Millipede

Worm

Centipede

Lobster

Crab

Limpet

Starfish

Sea Cucumber

Sea Urchin

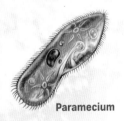

Paramecium

Cats and dogs seem to naturally understand each other, despite the different "languages" they may speak.

CHAPTER 1

PETS PEOPLE LOVE

All around the world, pets are part of the family. They make us happy. They make us laugh. They often amaze us. Sometimes they even protect their people. Pets make the world a brighter, better place!

america's most popular pets

1. Dogs
2. Cats
3. Hamsters
4. Fish
5. Mice

6. Guinea pigs
7. Birds
8. Snakes
9. Iguanas
10. Ferrets

77 million

Number of dogs kept as pets in the U.S.

TOP POOCH

Labrador retrievers have been rated America's favorite dog for more than 30 years! And it's no wonder: Labs are sweet-natured, smart and eager to please.

IT'S A DOG'S LIFE

Loyal and trusting, dogs are the world's most popular pet. They're happiest when they're part of a group—like a family. They need our attention and close friendship. And they deserve it!

ODD FELLOWS

Some pups get noticed! Like the puli, which looks more like a heap of yarn than a dog (top). They're quick learners. And they are good at herding if you happen to have a field of sheep! Then there's the mostly hairless Chinese crested dog (right). Some of them have soft, humanlike hair.

NEWLY POPULAR

The dachshund—aka a sausage dog—made the list of top 10 favorite canines in 2020. They love to snuggle. And they're very brave, so they also make great watchdogs!

BROTHER WOLF

All dogs are closely related to the gray wolf. About 15,000 years ago, some wolves were domesticated (doh-MESS-tuh-kay-ted). That means they began living with humans. Today, the wolf's closest kin are Chow Chows and Shiba Inus.

A LONGTIME FRIEND

The saluki has hung with people for at least 5,000 years. The breed got its start in the Middle East—some salukis even lived with Egyptian kings! Salukis are graceful dogs. They're also super-speedy, natural-born hunters.

CATS RULE!

Cats have lived with people for about 9,500 years. The ancient Egyptians even worshipped cats as gods. And sometimes our little kitties do think they rule the whole household!

58 million

Number of cats kept as pets in the U.S.

ALL MIXED UP

American shorthair cats are like the mutts of the feline world. They're a combo of many breeds. Some say they were brought to North America in the 1600s. If so, the ships they sailed on needed them—to work as rat catchers!

kitty love

Kittens are born blind and mostly deaf. That doesn't change till they're about 2 or 3 weeks old. All kittens are born with blue eyes. They're also beyond cute—and funny.

WATERPROOF!

It's said the Norwegian (nohr-WEE-jun) forest cat once ran with Vikings. "Weegies" are bundled up in an extra-thick, waterproof coat, and for good reason. When they were wild, these super-sweet cats prowled the snowy Norwegian woods.

BLUE-EYED BABES

Ragdolls (above) are cat-lovers' No. 1 favorite cat! They make great lap cats. Just pick one up and it goes limp—kind of like a rag doll! Another blue-eyed kitty is the Siamese. They're one of the oldest cat breeds there is.

WHERE'S MY TAIL?

The Manx looks like your everyday cat—except it's missing a tail! (Some do have a little stubby one.) Some say they come from the Isle of Man in the Irish Sea. That's how they got their name. But the Manx dislikes water as much as any other cat.

WHO NEEDS HAIR!

A cat without hair? Try these two breeds. Both prove even baldies are lovable. The sphinx (top) was named after a mysterious Egyptian statue called...the Sphinx. The Ukranian Levkoy (below) is a newer breed. They look like aliens, but they are very much from the planet Earth!

MORE PETS WE LOVE

**Dogs and cats take up the most human heart space.
But all of these animals also have plenty of fans!**

In Hawaii, it's against the law to have hamsters. Those in charge are afraid they'd get away. If they did, hamsters would take over the whole state!

HAM IT UP

Hamsters are America's most popular pet rodent. People mostly choose the Syrian hamster, which needs its own space. They don't share well with other hamsters, but they're friendly with people. So-called dwarf hamsters are also well loved. Three favorites: the dwarf Campbell's Russian, the dwarf winter white Russian and the Roborovski dwarf, which is teeny-tiny (not more than a couple inches).

GO FISH

Lots of people keep fish as pets. They don't take up much room. And the freshwater type is pretty easy to take care of. That's why goldfish (above) are always a top pick on the freshwater fish list. Tropical fish are another story. Most of them have intense, beautiful coloring, but they can live only in salt water. This makes them harder to care for. The flashy dottyback (at right) is a great fish for beginners. So are these two movie stars: the orange- and white-striped clown fish and the Pacific blue tang (below left)!

The betta is a showy freshwater fish. But watch out! It's also called the Siamese fighting fish. You can't put two of them together. If you do, they might battle to the death.

10.5 million

Number of U.S. households with fish

MICE ARE NICE!

A pet mouse? Why not? These rodents make excellent buddies. They can recognize their owners. They know their person's face, voice and smell. They're smart, and they love to hang out with you. And despite what your parents might think, they are actually extremely clean and can be trained to use a litter box. Plus, a pet mouse can be your own little sports buddy: They like to swim, jump, climb and balance on things.

There are more than 30 known species of mice, but the house mouse is the most popular one as a pet.

Excited guinea pigs "popcorn." That means they jump straight up and down. Sometimes they even turn in midair!

PICK A GUINEA PIG

Despite the name, these aren't part of the pig family—they're rodents. They may make little squeaky noises. They only sleep about four hours a day. They like being held and petted by people, but they don't care for living alone—they like to have at least one pal of their own kind to hang out with.

Birds can live very long lives—large parrots like macaws and Amazons can live up to 100 years!

smart alex

Alex was the name of a famous African gray. He lived from 1976 till 2007—31 years. He knew about 150 words, could count and was able to recognize different colors and shapes. He could also say things such as "See you tomorrow. I love you!"

BIRD BUSINESS

Many people like to keep pet birds, and the most popular kind is the parakeet (above). They're also known as "budgies." And they come in many bright colors. Want a bigger bird? The African gray is a fan favorite. Grays may be the smartest pet bird ever. They do need human time and attention, but it pays off: With a little training, many African grays can learn to talk. Lovebirds are also popular. They have loads of personality and are smart. Finches are small, pretty and need little attention. They're good for small homes. And the cockatiel (above right) wears quite a headdress! They can copy strange sounds, like the ring of a phone. Some also learn to talk.

SAVVY SNAKES

Get a corn snake and you've got a friend! These most-popular pet snakes (main image) are known for their friendly nature. They're easygoing and aren't hard to care for. Some pythons and boas also make good pets. Even big ones can be mellow and friendly. For example, the Kenyan sand boa (left) is a popular pick. These boas enjoy being handled. Plus, they come in many colors and patterns. And the hognose snake (below) has an upturned nose—giving it a look all its own.

Snakes can open their mouths very (very) wide—so they can eat things that may be as big as they are!

THE FANTASTIC FERRET

Cute, curious and smart: that describes this little guy pretty well. Ferrets sleep a lot. They also like to get out and roam every day. But beware! A ferret might take your stuff. The word "ferret" comes from the Latin language. It's a word that means "thief." That says it all!

Like many other reptiles, iguanas need UV light (like the kind from the sun)—and it has to shine directly onto their skin, not through a window or glass.

I WANNA IGUANA!

These mini-Godzillas are not cuddly. But once they trust you, they're fun to have around! Iguanas (ig-WAHN-ahs) can recognize their people and learn to come when you call them. These reptiles need lots of space, though. They're big climbers. You might even need a tree or two!

People first brought pet ferrets to America about 300 years ago.

CHAPTER 2

GIANTS OF THE ANIMAL KINGDOM

Talk about gigantic! In the wild animal kingdom, "big" has a meaning all its own. From fierce and powerful four-legged hunters to bugs as big as your back, these creatures are total showstoppers!

An African bush elephant can weigh around 12,000 pounds (5,443 kg)—that's as much as six horses!

THE BIGGEST OF THEIR KIND

These 10 animals are the mega-size models of their species.

Unlike most cats, Siberian tigers enjoy a good swim.

largest wild cat
SIBERIAN TIGER

Also known as the Amur tiger, these big cats are loners. They weight up to 475 pounds (215 kg) and can sometimes go for miles on their prowl for food. No two tigers have the same stripe pattern. Every one is different.

HOME TURF Russian Far East and some parts of China and North Korea

Baby elephants sometimes suck on their trunks like some kids suck on their thumbs!

largest land mammal
AFRICAN BUSH ELEPHANT

These massive mammals live 60 to 70 years. Their long trunks are used for digging, lifting and pushing. Sadly, some people kill elephants for their tusks, which are big teeth made of ivory.
HOME TURF Forests and grasslands of Africa

largest seal
SOUTHERN ELEPHANT SEAL

Southern elephant seals weigh as much as 8,800 pounds (4,000 kg). They are deep divers and can stay underwater without breathing for up to 20 minutes!
HOME TURF Antarctica

largest land mammal in the Americas
AMERICAN BISON

These great beasts were heavily hunted in the 1800s—and almost wiped out. But now there are many. They weigh up to 2,000 pounds (907 kg), about as much as two grand pianos.
HOME TURF Parts of western Canada and the United States

In the winter, bison use their shaggy heads to clear the snow and find plants to eat.

largest rodent
CAPYBARA

The capybara (ka-puh-BAA-ruh) is closely related to the guinea pig. This odd animal is a gentle giant, weighing about the same as a white-tailed deer, up to 146 pounds (66 kg). The females are often heavier. And they love getting together! Sometimes they even hang out in bunches of 100. But they need to watch out. Crocodiles and cougars enjoy them as dinner. **HOME TURF** Northern and central South America

Capybaras like cooling off in the water, often falling fast asleep there. Their webbed feet help them swim.

Kangaroos are awesome jumpers. Some can reach a height three times their own upright body—but they can't walk backward.

largest marsupial
RED KANGAROO

Don't make a male red kangaroo mad. He might lean back on his tail and try to punch you with his powerful hind legs. The males of this species are big and strong. They're as tall and as heavy as an average man, and they keep growing their whole lives. The females are smaller, faster and have a blue-toned coat. At birth, baby kangaroos are tinier than a single strawberry.
HOME TURF Inland Australia

Bats are the only mammals that can really fly.

name that 'roo!

Kangaroos are called by many names. A male is known as a jack, buck, boomer or old man. A female kangaroo is called a jill, roo, flyer or doe. And a baby kangaroo is called a joey.

largest bat
FLYING FOX

Their heads look foxlike, but these are no foxes. They're bats! If you saw one sailing above, you'd probably want to hide. Their wingspan can reach nearly as wide as the height of an average-size man. But they're lightweight critters. Their wings are made of thin, nearly see-through skin, so their total body weight is only about that of a 10-week-old kitten.
HOME TURF Mainland Asia, Papua New Guinea, Madagascar, Indonesia, Australia

largest bird
OSTRICH

How many toes would you say an ostrich has? You'd be right if you guessed four. They are the only bird with two toes on each foot. But they have a lot of something else—weight and speed. They can weigh more than 300 pounds (136 kg). And they are the fastest two-legged animal in the world: They can run as fast as 43 mph (69 kph). But they can't fly.
HOME TURF Across central Africa and parts of southern Africa

Ostriches have the largest eyes of any land animal. These gigantic eyes leave little room for a brain inside their skull. An ostrich's brain is actually smaller than one of its eyes!

The Chinese giant salamander is critically endangered, which means there aren't many left!

largest amphibian
CHINESE GIANT SALAMANDER

This odd amphibian (am-FIB-ee-uhn) can grow to almost 6 feet (1.9 m) long—about the height of a grown man—and are almost three times larger than North America's largest salamander, called the hellbender. They breathe through their skin and have short, chunky feet and bad eyesight.
HOME TURF Mountains of China

largest reptile
SALTWATER CROCODILE

You wouldn't want to get caught by one of these creatures! They're big and sneaky. They wait underwater, hoping to catch some dinner in their powerful jaws. Saltwater crocs are also strong swimmers. Sometimes they're seen far out in the ocean.

HOME TURF Northern Australia, eastern India and southeast Asia

17
feet (5 m)
The average length of a saltwater crocodile

land & sea creatures

Crabs and lobsters belong to the animal group called crustaceans (kruss-TAY-shunz). Here are the world's largest three.

JAPANESE SPIDER CRAB

The Japanese spider crab is the world's all-around biggest crustacean. It can grow 12 feet long (3.7 m) from claw to claw!

COCONUT CRAB

The coconut crab is the biggest land-living invertebrate in the world. It's named after its favorite food. It averages 40 inches (1 m) from top to tip.

AMERICAN LOBSTERS

Some American lobsters weigh even more than a 6-year-old boy. Like spider and coconut crabs, lobsters live in ocean waters.

JUMBOS OF THE DEEP

A lot of strange, big and beautiful creatures live in our oceans and seas.

Blue whales can hear each other at 1,000 miles (1,600 km) away. That's about the distance from Chicago to Denver!

GIANT MANTA RAY

This monster fish has a disc-shaped body. Its winglike fins can measure up to 29 feet (9 m) end to end. That's longer than the height of a two-story house!
HOME TURF Worldwide, but they usually prefer warmer waters like off the Yucatán Peninsula near Mexico

Of all the fish that scientists have studied, the giant manta ray has the biggest brain. Studies show they are good at using their memory. And they can recognize themselves in a mirror.

ORCA

The orca is the world's biggest dolphin. They are powerful hunters and killers, and will work together to take down even larger animals. That's why they're also known as killer whales.
HOME TURF All oceans, but more are found in the cold waters of places such as Alaska, Antarctica and Norway

Each orca group, or pod, has its own special sounds that others within the group recognize.

COLOSSAL SQUID

This guy wins the prize for the world's heaviest living squid at up to 2,000 pounds (907 kg). Its eyes are also huge—as big as soccer balls! They see well in the dark. They can also judge distances. These squid are mysterious. Few have ever been found to study.
HOME TURF Antarctic waters

BLUE WHALE

At up to 300,000 pounds (136,000 kg), the blue whale is the largest of all the animals. Its heart weighs as much as a small car. Its tongue is as heavy as one grown elephant! Blue whales have few natural enemies—but sometimes they are killed or hurt by big ships that run into them.
HOME TURF All oceans except the Arctic Ocean

WHALE SHARK

This biggest of all fish is humongous—longer than a bus! But it won't eat you. Whale sharks prefer the taste of very small fish and other tiny creatures. They don't chew or bite their prey. They just suck their meal straight in.
HOME TURF All warmwater seas, such as along Australia's central west coast

Mother whale sharks leave their babies once they are born. Only one out of 10 survives.

A colossal squid's eyes don't just make it easier to see in the dark. They cast a glow on objects down there in the deep. This squid can see a glow around an object that would be as far away as the length of a whole football field.

1 million

Estimated number of animal species that live in the ocean today

SLITHER, SLIDE & CRAWL

These big animals get around in water or on land faster than you might think!

The Komodo dragon's forked yellow tongue helps it smell possible food. But if an enemy comes near, Mr. Komodo will throw up all his food to get away faster.

Anacondas kill their prey by grabbing it and holding it underwater till it drowns.

GREEN ANACONDA

These snakes aren't the longest in the world. But at up to 154 pounds (70 kg) they are the heaviest. Females weigh even more than males. They lurk in slow-moving rivers, streams and swamps.
HOME TURF Trinidad and South America

KOMODO DRAGON

These reptiles are like a flashback to the way-long-ago past. Their species has been on the planet for millions of years. And at 8 feet (2.4 m) long, no lizard is bigger. They're also dangerous. Unlike most lizards, they have a venomous bite.
HOME TURF Some Indonesian islands

Baby leatherbacks born in warm nests turn out to be female. If the nest is cooler, male babies are born.

150 million years

Leatherback sea turtles are one of the oldest species on Earth—they have survived since the time of the dinosaurs!

LEATHERBACK SEA TURTLE

Meet the largest and heaviest turtle alive at up to 7 feet (2.1 m) long and more than 1,500 pounds (680 kg)! Leatherback shells are smooth and leatherlike. They have little spines in their throats that point downward. These spines let jellyfish go down the hatch—but they can't get out.

HOME TURF Mild and warm waters all over the world, including coastal waters off the U.S., Puerto Rico and the Virgin Islands

BIG IN A SMALL WORLD

There are more insects on Earth than any other kind of animal. Scientists have named 900,000 different species. They suspect there are millions more waiting to be discovered. Here are some of the biggest ones we know about.

largest insect
ZHAO'S CHINESE WALKING STICK

If you're not a fan of gigantic, creepy bugs, run! This monster looks like a large tree branch, but it lives and breathes. Its full name is very hard to pronounce: Phryganistria chinensis Zhao!
HOME TURF China's Guangxi Province

largest butterfly
QUEEN ALEXANDRA BIRDWING BUTTERFLY

Introducing a beautiful giant! The females are bigger, but the males stand out more. Their wings are a deep blue-green and yellow. The females are brown. This species is so rare that little is known about it.
HOME TURF Forests of Papua New Guinea

2 monster moths

ATLAS MOTH
These gentle giants are the largest moths in the world. Their beauty could stop a crowd—but they have no mouth, so they can't eat. Once out of the cocoon, they live only one or two weeks.
HOME TURF Asian forests

HERCULES MOTH
Another big beautiful moth without a mouth, it also dies within two weeks. But as a caterpillar it can live for three months.
HOME TURF Northern Australia and New Guinea

largest cockroach
MEGALOBLATTA LONGIPENNIS

If you don't like bugs, beware! The megaloblatta (meg-uh-loh-BLAH-tuh) could take up almost all of your forehead. Like most cockroaches, it's nocturnal—it only comes out at night.
HOME TURF Mexico, Costa Rica, Panama, Ecuador and Peru

largest spider
GIANT HUNTSMAN SPIDER

Spiders belong to an animal group called arachnids (uh-RAK-nidz). This one has venom, or poison, in its fangs (but not enough to kill you).
HOME TURF Laos

the goliaths

Goliath was a huge giant in the Bible. That's how these creatures got their names.

GOLIATH BIRDEATER

These spiders have venom in their inch-long fangs. They are wicked hunters and have sharp-ended leg hairs that they shoot into their enemy's eyes and skin.
HOME TURF South American rain forests

ROYAL GOLIATH BEETLE

This black-and-white bug can grow almost as large as an adult human hand. Their "royal" dinners include tree sap, bark and fruit.
HOME TURF Many countries in Africa

GOLIATH FROG

This is the biggest frog in the world, with an appetite to match. These amphibians eat things such as worms, insects, small crabs and snakes—even smaller frogs.
HOME TURF West Africa near the Equator

CHAPTER 3
SMALL BUT MIGHTY

Our world is full of millions of itsy-bitsy animals—some so tiny you can't really even see them! But despite their miniature stature, these little guys contribute a lot to our world.

Most hummingbirds can beat their wings 60 to 80 times a second. That humming sound their wings make gave them their name!

8 LITTLE GUYS YOU'LL LOVE

Don't overlook these cuties! Here are some of our favorite miniature creatures.

The gray mouse lemur gets its name from its small size and mouselike appearance.

smallest primate
GRAY MOUSE LEMUR

Primates are animals with hands and feet. Humans are primates. So are monkeys, apes and lemurs. And the gray mouse lemur is the tiniest primate of all. Around 10 inches (25 cm) long, it weighs only a little more than 2 ounces (57g)—that's just as much as two slices of bread!
HOME TURF Madagascar, an island near Africa

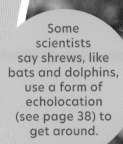

Some scientists say shrews, like bats and dolphins, use a form of echolocation (see page 38) to get around.

smallest mammal (by weight)
ETRUSCAN SHREW

At just 0.05 ounces (1.4 g), this little fellow weighs less than a dime! But it speeds around like a miniature race car. This constant speed means a shrew needs to keep its energy up, so it's a nonstop eater, too. Favorite foods include insects, larvae, lizards and rodents. Yum!
HOME TURF Europe, Malaysia and North Africa

smallest marsupial
LONG-TAILED PLANIGALE

This animal has a very tiny body. It weighs about 0.15 ounces (4 g), or about as much as a board game die. It's also very flat, so it can get into cracks in rocks and the ground to find food.
HOME TURF Australia

Male pudú grow antlers like other deer. But as pudú stand barely a foot tall, their antlers are only a few inches long.

smallest deer
PUDÚ

If you have a small dog, you can imagine the size of the tiniest deer in the world. At around 13 inches (33 cm) tall, it's about as tall as a ruler, and weighs about 10 pounds (4.5 kg). It likes to hide in rain forests, where it can eat plants growing close to the ground.
HOME TURF Chile and Argentina

This little spider is named in part for its muffin-top shape.

smallest spider
SPARKLEMUFFIN

Who would name a spider sparklemuffin? Well, its real name is the Australian peacock spider, and it has a "tummy flap" that looks like a fan of peacock feathers. Its amazing red-and-blue markings really sparkle! How teeny is a sparklemuffin? Try measuring the thin side edge of a credit card. This tiny thing is smaller than that—just about 0.3 inches (.8 cm)! It belongs to the group called jumping spiders, and can leap over 20 times its body size.
HOME TURF Australia

smallest mammal (by size)
BUMBLEBEE BAT

Do bats scare you? Even if they do, this one shouldn't. It's hardly bigger than a bumblebee—and it doesn't sting. The bumblebee bat is the smallest of all mammals, less than 2 inches (5 cm) long and 0.07 ounces (2 g), or about as much as one playing card! These micro mammals live in forest caves near rivers. They form groups of up to 100. And they never fly far from home.
HOME TURF Thailand and Myanmar

The bumblebee bat was discovered in 1973 by a scientist named Kitti Thonglongya, so it's also called Kitti's hog-nosed bat.

what is echolocation?

Bats and other animals (like whales) use echolocation to get around. They send out sounds from their noses and mouths. When these sounds hit an object (say, a tree) they bounce back to the bat's ears. That echo tells bats about the object's size, shape and location so they won't run into things in the dark.

Bee hummingbird babies are born featherless and blind.

smallest tortoise
SPECKLED PADLOPER TORTOISE

Also known as the speckled cape tortoise or just the speckled tortoise, adults are just around 2.5 inches (6 cm) long (about the size of a packet of sugar) and weigh around 4.5 ounces (128 g). "Padloper" means "path walker" in the South African language of Afrikaans. Their name isn't surprising; padlopers make little pathways wherever they go. They are a near-threatened species, although some people still keep them as pets.

HOME TURF Parts of Namibia and South Africa

Padlopers have five toes on their fore feet, while many of their relatives just have four toes.

smallest bird
BEE HUMMINGBIRD

So tiny and cute! They lay coffee bean-sized eggs, and the nests they build are no bigger than the width of a quarter. They're not quite as long as two small end-to-end paper clips and weigh just around 0.06 ounces (1.7 g). Because they're so small, they're often mistaken for insects. But the bee hummingbird is fast enough to keep up with a car moving along a city street.

HOME TURF Cuba

REAL-LIFE FAIRY TALES

These little animals have names straight out of a storybook.

The fairy armadillo gets its pink color from the blood vessels in its shell.

VERNAL POOL FAIRY SHRIMP

"Vernal" means having to do with springtime. During rainy vernal days, little ponds form. This is where these tiny see-through shrimp—which measure only between 0.5 to 2 inches (1.3 cm-5 cm)—get their start. They swim upside down, looking for food.

HOME TURF Vernal pools in California and Oregon

Fairy shrimp are relatives to lobsters and crabs.

PINK FAIRY ARMADILLO

Sometimes called the sand-swimmer, it can dig very fast into sandy ground, where it spends most of its life. They are around 4 inches (10 cm) long and weigh just about 4 ounces (113 g). Pink fairies only come out at night.

HOME TURF Parts of South America

RED-BACKED FAIRY-WREN

There are many fairy-wren species, but these birds are the smallest. They weigh around 0.28 ounces (8 g) and are around 4.5 inches (11 cm) in length. They build dome-shaped nests in well-hidden spots. These nests are then lined with feathers and soft grasses—all the better for their even teensier babies to hatch.

HOME TURF Northern and eastern Australia

The eye-catching red feathers on the back of the male red-backed fairy wren are helpful in attracting a mate.

Fairy wasps are useful insects. Many insects eat farm crops. But fairy wasps destroy the eggs of these pests. This helps farmers a lot!

FAIRY WASP

These itty-bitty insects are no bigger than the head of a pin—they are less than ¼-inch (0.6 cm) long! They have feathery wings and float around like specks of dust. One fairy wasp species is called Tinkerbella nana. They were named after the famous fairy, Tinkerbell, from *Peter Pan*.

HOME TURF Worldwide, except Antarctica

us & them

Ever notice those feelers on some animals' heads? They're called antennae. Humans would look pretty weird with those! But shrimp and wasps really need them. They use their antennae to "taste" and "smell" the world around them. We people use our mouths and noses for that!

THREE LITTLE PYGMIES

You've heard the tale of the three little pigs, right? Now here's the story on these three little pygmies!

The little pygmy-possum is also known as the Tasmanian pigmy possum.

LITTLE PYGMY POSSUM

These marsupials are just about 3 inches long (8 cm) and weigh around 0.3 ounces (8.5 g), and they live in trees. Unfortunately, these critters are at risk of becoming endangered. Wild cats hunt them, and in January 2020, a raging fire hit an island they call home. Later, scientists made a happy discovery: They found some little pygmy possums still alive.
HOME TURF Mainly Tasmania and Kangaroo Island, Australia

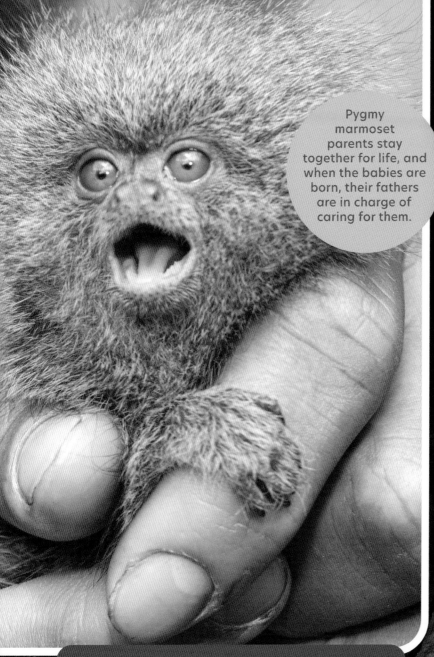

Pygmy marmoset parents stay together for life, and when the babies are born, their fathers are in charge of caring for them.

SOUTHERN PYGMY SQUID

These are the smallest of their kind. In length, they range from 0.16 to 0.7 inches (0.4 cm to 2 cm) long and weigh under half an ounce (14 g). While they may be mini, they are fierce predators that feast on small crustaceans. They make glue in their bodies, which is important to their lives. Females use the glue to stick their eggs to the undersides of seagrass. Pygmy squids also use their glue to hide themselves under the seagrass. When a shrimp washes by, the squid jumps out to attack it. Dinner is served!

HOME TURF Southwestern Pacific Ocean

Male Southern pygmy squid have 10 suckers on their tentacles.

PYGMY MARMOSET

A marmoset is a very tiny monkey. Pygmy marmosets grow up to 6 inches (15 cm) tall and scamper through the trees much like squirrels do, but they can't hang from trees the way other monkeys can. Their tails, which are used primarily for balance, are longer than their bodies, and they can turn their heads backward to watch for enemies.

HOME TURF Rain forests in South America

term to know

A **predator** (PREHD-uh-tuhr) is an animal that eats other animals.

MORE SMALL STUFF TO ADORE

Some of these critters have names almost too hard to say. And they're not so easy to see, either!

ROYAL ANTELOPE

Take a look at the world's smallest antelope. You might not get another chance; they are only 10 inches (25 cm) tall and weigh between 5 and 7 pounds (2–3 kg)—about as tall as a cereal box and lighter than a big jug of milk! These little animals are shy and nocturnal. They live on the floor of dense rain forests, where their reddish-brown fur blends right in.
HOME TURF Western Africa

Male royal antelope grow a teeny little pair of cone-shaped black horns.

The antelope was a sacred, or religiously important, animal in many very old cultures. It was often associated with the moon. Two gods of the Hindu religion rode in chariots pulled by antelopes. And in Liberian myths, the royal antelope is a symbol of wisdom and speed. They do run away from danger very quickly!

SPRUCE-FIR MOSS SPIDER

Do you know what a tarantula is? It's a big hairy, scary type of spider. The spruce-fir moss spider is one of those. But this species does not fit in the "big" group. Rather, it's one of the smallest tarantulas around and usually only measures between 0.10 to 0.15 inches (0.25-0.4 cm) long—about the size of a BB pellet. These spiders are mountain climbers. They're found on high peaks where spruce and fir trees grow, but as humans have cut down their trees they've become endangered.

HOME TURF Parts of Tennessee, Virginia and North Carolina

These spiders construct tube-shaped webs to help lure prey.

The Jaragua dwarf gecko is thought to be the smallest reptile in the world.

JARAGUA DWARF GECKO

The Jaragua dwarf gecko was only discovered in 2001. It was found in a place biologists have studied for hundreds of years. That proves how small this gecko is! It measures less than 1 inch (2.5 cm) from nose to tail tip and weighs 0.00455 of an ounce (0.13 g)—less than a drop of rain! It is the smallest of all small lizards.

HOME TURF Caribbean Islands

term to know

A **biologist** (bi-OL-uh-jist) is a scientist who studies living things.

Despite being little, paedophryne amauensis frogs live fairly long—up to five years.

PAEDOPHRYNE AMAUENSIS FROG

Just forget trying to say the name of this frog species! All you need to know is that they are the world's smallest vertebrates at just 0.30 inches (0.8 cm) long. That means they're super tiny. Two of them could probably sit back-to-back on a dime! They hide in leaf litter on the forest floor. That may be why they were not discovered until 2009.
HOME TURF Papua New Guinea

The paedocypris never seems to grow up: Even fully grown its body looks much like a newly hatched fish!

PAEDOCYPRIS FISH

The tiny paedocypris (pee-dah-SIP-riss) belongs to the carp family. At under a half-inch (1.3 cm) long, they are the smallest known mature fish specimen. They are also endangered. They live only in swampy forest waters. The swamp water has a kind of bubbly acid, like soda pop. Paedocypris can only survive in this kind of water, but these waters are fast drying up.
HOME TURF Southeast Asian islands of Borneo, Sumatra and Bintan

CHAPTER 4

HOME ON THE MOUNTAIN & IN THE WOODS

Whether up on a high peak or hidden in a forest, these animals manage to make the most of the places they live.

ON TOP OF THE WORLD

Many animals live on mountains, where they face icy temperatures and little food. Here are some of the highest dwellers of all.

Unlike other big cats, snow leopards can't roar. They do have a call, but it's more of a piercing yell.

SNOW LEOPARD

These rare big cats thrive at high altitudes. Their thick fur keeps them warm and their giant paws are like snowshoes that allow them to travel more than 25 miles (40 km) each night. They can jump six times their own body length in one leap!
HOME TURF Mongolia, Himalayas and other Asian mountain ranges

YAK

No mammal lives on higher ground than the yak, which regularly climbs 20,000 feet (6,100 m) and beyond. These domesticated dudes live peacefully with people. They have shaggy, two-layer woolly coats that allow them to enjoy swimming in freezing waters and dense horns that let them break through snow and ice to get to the plants growing underneath.

HOME TURF Central Asia

HIMALAYAN JUMPING SPIDER

This spider's scientific name means "standing above everything." That makes sense, since these eight-legged crawlers have even been found on the surface of the world's highest peak: Mount Everest.

HOME TURF Himalayan mountain range in Asia

Butter made from yak's milk is used to fuel oil lamps in Tibet.

MOUNTAIN GOAT

These furry fellas aren't really goats; they're relatives of cows and antelopes. And they're very sure-footed, even at altitudes of 13,000 feet (4,000 m) or more. You can tell the age of one by counting the rings on its horns.

HOME TURF Alaska, and parts of the western United States and Canada

The dads are called "billies." The moms are called "nannies." And the kids are called "kids"!

The Pokémon character Pikachu is loosely based on the pika.

PIKA

Pikas like open rocky mountainsides high above the tree line. They also live in grassy meadows at altitudes of 8,200 feet (2,500 m) and above. They have fur on the bottoms of their feet, which is good for cold weather! And they are known for their loud chirps, squeaks and screams.

HOME TURF Western United States and Canada

CHIRU

This graceful mammal is also called the Tibetan antelope or gazelle, but it's not actually related to either. It grazes on flat, wide-open ground high in the mountains. Only the males have horns, which start developing when they are young.

HOME TURF Southwestern China

During mating season, the male's face and front legs appear black, in sharp contrast to the rest of its fur.

the hunt goes on

The chiru is endangered. A person could go to jail for killing or harming one. But they are still being hunted for their silky hair, called shahtoosh. People use the wool to secretly make shawls and scarves. Then these items sell for lots of money—like $15,000! Three to five chirus must be killed to make one shawl.

Andean crested ducks in the high Andes have yellow-orange eyes, while in southern countries, such as Chile and Argentina, they have red eyes.

LAMMERGEIER

The lammergeier is a cold-world predator, whose name in Spanish (quebrantahusos) means "bone breaker." It's also sometimes called the bearded vulture. This big bird builds its nests on high cliff edges thousands of feet up in the mountains.
HOME TURF Mountainous regions of Europe, Asia and Africa

KIANG

Also called the Tibetan wild ass, they search for food in groups. While some of these groups are as small as five members, others might have as many as 400—all led by an older female. These scramblers are fine at altitudes from 13,000 to 30,000 feet (4,000 m to 9,000 m).
HOME TURF Nepal, India and parts of China

ANDEAN CRESTED DUCK

Most crested birds have a big obvious crest on their heads, but it's hard to see on these ducks. They live near rivers, lakes and marshes high in the Andes mountain range.
HOME TURF Peru, Bolivia, Chile and Argentina

To defend themselves against wolves, kiangs form a circle, lower their heads and violently kick out.

WILD THINGS

Woodlands and forests are home to too many animal species to count. They depend on trees for shelter to survive, so saving their trees saves them as well!

At up to 3 feet (0.9 m) long and upwards of 70 pounds (32 kg), beavers are the world's second-largest rodent after the capybara.

BEAVER

Check out those teeth! They're long, strong, orange and never stop growing! Their teeth and long claws help them build dams and dome-shaped homes called lodges. Their tails are covered in black scales and their webbed back feet make them splendid swimmers.
HOME TURF Most of North America

GIANT PANDA BEAR

People love pandas! But in the wild they can be deadly. They eat mostly bamboo stalks, so that means they need sharp teeth and strong jaws to cut through these tough plants. They weigh upwards of 100 pounds (45 kg) and are great swimmers and climbers, but they're pretty lazy and spend most of their days eating and sleeping.
HOME TURF Mountainous bamboo forests of southwestern China

When they're born, giant pandas are furless, pink and blind; they don't develop their familiar black-and-white coloring until they are about 3 weeks old.

The ermine's silky fur was long prized and worn by kings and queens.

ERMINE

Also known as short-tailed weasels, their white fur (with a black-tipped tail) gives these little guys a real wow factor. But that's only their winter coat. When the weather gets warm they turn brown.

HOME TURF Across Eurasia and North America

GOLDEN PHEASANT

The male of this species is one flashy fellow, with a sunny yellow crest atop those red and orange feathers. They are not strong flyers. In fact, they mostly peck away on the forest floor. And if these birds get too much sun, their colors fade fast!

HOME TURF Mountain forests in China; some are also in the United Kingdom

After birth, baby koalas (called joeys) climb up into their mother's pouch. They stay there for about six months.

KOALA

Koalas are not bears. They're marsupials! They snooze 18 to 22 hours a day. When they wake up, they eat huge amounts of eucalyptus leaves, and then go back to sleep. Meanwhile, their bodies are hard at work, digesting those leaves.

HOME TURF Eastern and southeastern Australia

MAKING SCENTS

What do you notice first about these animals? No doubt it's their very notable noses. Every one of these forest-dwellers relies on its schnoz to stay alive!

MOUNTAIN TAPIR

Out of four tapir species, this one has lived on Earth the longest—about 60 million years! It's also called the Andean tapir or the woolly tapir. This creature's elephantlike trunk is useful for many things—such as grabbing tasty leaves. Their babies have a "watermelon"-patterned coat to help them blend into their surroundings. Sadly, they are an endangered species primarily due to habitat loss.
HOME TURF Mountain forests and high plateaus in northern Peru, Ecuador and Colombia

Some people say a wild boar will eat anything that fits in its mouth!

WILD BOAR

Boars have terrible eyesight, but their long snouts pick up smells well. They're also excellent athletes: Boars run fast and are great swimmers. They sleep 12 hours a day, and then finally come out at night. That's when they snort around and find food! Their curled tusks give them a special look.
HOME TURF Forests throughout Asia, Europe and in northwest Africa

The tapir's closest relatives are the rhinoceros and the horse.

Echidnas have the lowest body temperature of any mammal—around 89 F (32 C).

STAR-NOSED MOLE

These little critters have a super-sharp sense of touch. That's thanks to those 22 pink pointy things at the end of their snouts, called tentacles. They all come in handy when you live mostly underground in the dark. And talk about nosy: These tiny moles are also the only mammals that can smell underwater.

HOME TURF Northeastern North America (Quebec, Canada, south to the Appalachian Mountains)

Star-nosed moles eat faster than any other mammal!

ECHIDNA

Also known as the spiny anteater, the echidna has porcupinelike spines, a birdlike beak and a kangaroo-esque pouch. They are one of only two mammals that lay eggs instead of giving birth to live babies (the platypus is the other). Another odd thing: The echidna uses its nose to grab bugs from the forest floor.

HOME TURF Tasmania and Australia

100,000

Number of "touch sensors" on a star-nosed mole, which gives them a super-amazing sense of touch. These sensors take up about as much space as the tip of a person's finger and are five times better at feeling things than our hands.

5–7 months

How long bears hibernate

MEET THE MEAT EATERS

A temperate forest is one whose trees drop their leaves in the fall. A lot of meat eaters, or carnivores, live in these woods, where they find plenty of prey among the varied plants and vegetation.

Grizzlies belong to the brown bear family. Brown bears are also found in Europe and Russia.

GRIZZLY BEAR

These heavyweight hunters are usually loners. They eat small creatures such as mice, as well as much bigger prey, even deer and moose. They also munch on berries, roots, grass and plants. Whatever they eat, they eat a lot—up to 90 pounds (41 kg) of food per day. When winter comes, they head to their hideaway for a long, sleeplike state called hibernation. Be sure to avoid their front claws; they can be up to 4 inches (10 cm) long!

HOME TURF Parts of Canada and the western United States

GOSHAWK

The goshawk is a raptor, or bird of prey, known for its speed and patience. (It can spend up to an hour following its prey.) This fierce hunter flies among close-growing trees, and can swoop down and grab a fox for dinner, no problem! No wonder one writer called the goshawk a "jet fighter with flapping wings!"

HOME TURF Newfoundland, Canada, to Alaska and south

The U.S. Navy named one of its jets after this bird: the T45-Goshawk.

term to know

Prey is an animal hunted by other animals for food.

GRAY WOLF

This big predator has a spooky howl. The wolf pack uses these sounds to communicate. A wolf can kill a large deer by itself, but hunting with buddies is easier. At mealtime, the leaders—known as the alphas—get to eat first.

HOME TURF North America, eastern Europe and Russia

The gray wolf is known as the timber wolf in North America. In the Arctic, it's called the white wolf.

Humans share around 98% of our DNA with gorillas, making them one of our closest relatives.

MOUNTAIN GORILLA

These are powerful animals. One mountain gorilla can be as strong as 20 men! And they're massive, weighing between 300 and 500 pounds (136–227 kg). They live in small family groups. On cold nights, they cuddle up close. At about age 12, male gorillas start growing silver hair on their back and hips; that's why they're called silverbacks.

HOME TURF Rwanda, Uganda and Democratic Republic of the Congo

ANIMALS OF THE RAIN FOREST

More than 3 million different kinds of creatures call tropical rain forests home. In fact, while rain forests take up only a very small part of Earth, they contain about half of the world's animal species.

JAGUAR

As the biggest cat species in the Americas, the jaguar rules! Their spotted fur keeps them well-hidden in the dense forest growth. Swimming comes easily for them, and they usually live near water such as lakes, rivers and wetlands. And they love a good nighttime hunt.
HOME TURF Amazon basin in South America and some parts of Central America

Jaguars are loners! Generally they travel alone, with males and females only coming together to mate.

MATA MATA

This odd-looking turtle has a shell that looks like tree bark, and its head looks like a big leaf. Mostly, they hide underwater, where they bury themselves into the soggy fallen leaves on river bottoms and stream beds. To eat, they suck up tiny fish like a vacuum—without even chewing.
HOME TURF Amazon and Orinoco Basins, South America

In Spanish, mata mata translates to "kill, kill."

2 amazing birds

AFRICAN DWARF KINGFISHER
Tiny and as colorful as a jewel, the African dwarf kingfisher is less than 4 inches (10 cm) long. Despite its name, it hardly ever eats fish. It watches closely for insects, lizards and frogs and makes a dive for dinner.
HOME TURF Numerous central African countries and western coastal areas

SCARLET IBIS
After it is born, the baby scarlet ibis has mostly dark grey feathers, but over time, its feathers turn bright red as it feeds on red crabs.
HOME TURF South America, Trinidad and Tobago

GOLDEN POISON DART FROG

All poison dart frogs are just that—poisonous! But the golden dart frog is the most deadly, with enough poison in their skin to kill 10 grown men. They're brightly colored, but you still might not spot them in their woodsy world. Hold up a small paper clip—that's about how tall they grow.

HOME TURF A small area of Colombia's rain forest

crazy bugs!

UNICORN PRAYING MANTIS

The unicorn praying mantis has a horn on its head—like a unicorn! They can grow as big as a human hand, but who wants to hold it?

HOME TURF Brazil

LEAF CUTTER ANT

Leaf cutter ants carry big chunks of leaves to their nests. Growths on the leaves then become food for the ants.

HOME TURF Central and South America

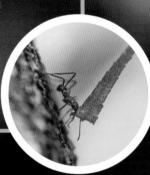

Poison dart frogs use their long tongues to catch prey. Their eyesight is better than most frogs, so they rarely miss a strike!

The emperor tamarin got its name from a man with a big bushy mustache: Wilhelm II, the German emperor and the king of Prussia, who ruled from 1888 to 1918.

EMPEROR TAMARIN

What kind of animal is this? If you guessed monkey, you're right! These whiskery creatures have claws on all their fingers and toes—except their big toes. They live in family groups, and a father emperor tamarin helps birth the new babies. Once the baby is born, he then washes it clean.

HOME TURF Brazil, Bolivia and Peru

THREE-TOED SLOTH

These cuties sleep up to 20 hours a day. Even awake, they barely move at all. In fact, they're slower than any other mammal on Earth. Sloths have weak hind legs and have to pull themselves along using their front claws. Their bellies scrape the ground as they move.

HOME TURF Central and South America

Sloths spend about 90% of their lives hanging upside down from trees, and can turn their heads almost all the way around.

DRACO LIZARD

It's not a bird! It's not a plane! It's a flying lizard! The draco has long, skin-covered ribs on the sides of its body. As it leaps, it reaches back with its arms to pull these "wings" open. Then it glides through the air. What an awesome sight!

HOME TURF Borneo, the Philippines, Southeast Asia and into southern India

These reptiles are also known as flying dragons.

CHAPTER 5

LIFE ON THE GRASSLANDS, PLAINS & DESERTS

From teeny fish to big cats, these amazing animals have all adapted to living in some wide-open spaces.

African lions are very social. They live in groups of about 15 lions, called prides.

ON THE SAVANNA

The African savanna is one of the largest grassland areas in the world. It covers about half of the continent, and is home to some strange and wonderful creatures that most of us have only seen in zoos and pictures.

These beautiful animals can go for days without drinking water. It's hard for them to get their heads close to the ground to take a sip!

GIRAFFE

A giraffe's foot is about as big as a dinner plate. Its tongue is about as long as the body of a dachshund. And its heart is bigger than any other land mammal's—nearly the size of a watermelon. And of course, giraffes are the world's tallest animals, standing up to 20 lanky feet (6 m)!

HOME TURF East and southern Africa

HIPPOPOTAMUS

If you want to find a hippo, check the water! That's where they spend most of their time. A hippo sinks most of its body underwater, so only its eyes and nostrils show. That way they can cool off, breathe and watch for enemies all at once! They may look cute but they can be mean.
HOME TURF East Africa

At birth, an average baby weighs 100 pounds (45 kg). That's about the same as a 13-year-old human boy.

GNU

The gnu (NEW) is a big, shaggy-maned mammal known for its long-distance travel. Their migration (moving from place to place) lasts a year as they search for fresh grasslands. Sometimes as many as 1 million gnus travel together, often with gazelles and zebras.
HOME TURF Central, southern and eastern Africa

Spotted hyenas got a lot of attention as some of the villains in the movie *The Lion King.*

SPOTTED HYENA

Hyenas look a lot like dogs, but they are more closely related to cats. Spotted hyenas are dangerous, and can run long distances without tiring. The spotted hyena's super-strong jaws can crush a giraffe leg with one snap. They are also known as laughing hyenas, for the sounds they make, but they're far from silly. Actually, they are some of the smartest animals in the region.
HOME TURF Central, south and east Africa

all in the stripes

Every zebra alive has a stripe pattern all its own—no two have exactly the same. Each zebra species also has a basic pattern that tells what kind it is.

PLAINS ZEBRA

There are three zebra species, but the plains zebra is the most common. It's also the smallest, and the only kind on the savanna. Scientists think having stripes helps protect zebras from predators because when zebras stand close together, it's hard to pick out one from the herd.
HOME TURF Eastern and southern Africa

PANGOLIN

These shy mammals are named from the Malay word for "roller"—they curl up in a ball to protect themselves. They use their long claws to dig into termite mounds for a meal. Pangolins have no teeth so to break up food, they swallow rocks!
HOME TURF Southern, central and eastern Africa, and parts of Asia

A single pangolin can eat 70 million ants and termites each year!

Male bustards really show off to attract the female birds. One way they do this is to puff up their beautiful neck feathers like a balloon.

THOMSON'S GAZELLE

Nicknamed "tommies," these graceful animals are a type of antelope. When an enemy chases, a gazelle can change direction fast to escape! They can also jump straight up, over and over, which is called "pronking" or "stotting." They swish their tails back and forth like a windshield wiper.
HOME TURF East Africa

TERMITE

The hot, dry savanna is a termite's perfect home. Here, they build huge mounds to live in. Thousands of them hang out together in these mounds. It's a good place to hide—which is helpful, since lots of desert animals like to eat them!
HOME TURF Every continent except Antarctica

Termite groups are ruled by a queen termite. Queens can live as long as 45 years. That's if the worker termites don't lick her to death!

KORI BUSTARD

This is one big, heavy bird! Kori bustards weigh up to 40 pounds (18 kg) and can stand 5 feet (1.5 m) tall. It can fly, but it's not easy to lift all that weight. So the bustard keeps to the ground unless it needs to escape danger.
HOME TURF Southern Africa

An aardvark can eat as many as 50,000 termites or ants in a single night.

AARDVARK

They love to dine on termites, but take in a lot of dirt and sand as they munch, which wears on their teeth. Luckily, those teeth never stop growing. Aardvarks also have looong, sticky tongues—up to 12 inches (30 cm)!
HOME TURF Throughout sub-Saharan Africa

Scientists discovered that dung beetles watch the stars above to find their way home.

SOUTHERN GROUND HORNBILL

The southern ground hornbill has a giant beak, or bill. It looks like it has dark curly eyelashes, but those are actually feathers that help keep dust out of its eyes. One favorite food: dung beetles!
HOME TURF Southern Africa

DUNG BEETLE

Dung is animal droppings—poop. That's mainly what these beetles eat. Some roll the droppings into a ball. At the hottest part of the day, they crawl up on their poop ball to cool off their feet. Then they push it home so their young can eat it too. Both parents care for their kids.
HOME TURF All continents except Antarctica

Male southern ground hornbills are *loud*! Sometimes people think their deep-throated call is a lion roaring.

BLACK MAMBA

These reptiles are wickedly fierce and dangerous. They can grow up to 14 feet (4.3 m). Their venom can take out a full-grown human. No wonder they have a reputation as the world's most deadly snake! Black mambas usually run from danger, but if an enemy bothers them, they may strike over and over.

HOME TURF Sub-Saharan Africa

Despite its name, the black mamba is actually gray or dark brown. The "black" comes from the dark color inside their mouths—which hopefully you'll never see!

How fast can you run? Adults who are not trained as athletes can run about 10 miles an hour (16 kph). A southern ground hornbill (left) prefers walking, but it can fly about 18 miles an hour (29 kph). At top speed, a black mamba can slither away at 12.5 mph (20 kph).

WEAVERS & WEB BUILDERS

The African savanna is full of weavers. These creatures use twigs, plant parts or spider's silk to build their homes—no loom required!

Village weavers are so named because they often nest in or near African villages.

SOCIABLE WEAVER

With their neutral-colored feathers, these birds are not at all flashy, but they sure love a party. Sociable weavers hang out happily in huge groups. And they weave massive nests. Their homes hold as many as 100 weaver families together. From afar these nests look like big clumps of hay in a tree.

VILLAGE WEAVER

Nests for these yellow-and-black birds are always built by the guys. They weave together strips of palm leaves and other plants. Unlike many nests, the entrance here is on the bottom. And they're really hard to build. It takes about 9 to 15 hours to finish one nest!

African electrical companies have sociable weaver problems. These birds love to build their gigantic nests on electricity poles. Sometimes the nests are so heavy, the poles collapse.

GOLDEN SILK ORB-WEAVER

Lots of spiders weave, but the golden silk orb-weaver's web is huge. While many spider webs are gone in a few days, theirs sometimes last for years. These eight-legged wonders are also known as banana spiders or giant wood spiders, but they're not really giant—they grow to be only about 2 inches (5 cm) long. Golden silk spiders are harmless to people, but even small birds need to watch out!

Golden silks are the oldest spider species alive today. Scientists have found fossils dating back 165 million years!

building an orb

Orb-web builders let out threads of thin, strong silk. They attach strands to sturdy objects like a branch. Then they weave one circle inside another. At the center is sticky silk. When prey gets stuck, the spider rushes in and bites it to death.

Silver vlei spiders have very small fangs, but are hesitant to bite unless absolutely necessary.

SILVER VLEI SPIDER

A vlei (FLEI) is marshy, low-lying ground. And these spiders love a good vlei. Their orb-webs are often found strung in wet grasses. Wherever they build, it's usually near water—where lots of bugs will fly by, get caught in the web and wind up as lunch.

BIG CATS!

The animal world includes thousands of cat species. But there are very few so-called big cats. The African savanna is home to three of them. And all are paws-itively showstoppers!

No animal hunts a lion for food. But spotted hyenas are a lion's problem. They hunt in packs and go after the same foods that lions eat, which can limit supply.

LION

Hunting big prey is the name of the game for this cat. The male, with its regal mane, is often called the king of beasts, but it's the females that do most of the hunting. They bring down gazelles, zebras and gnus. In hunting bigger prey, like giraffes, the males may sometimes join in. Otherwise, their job is protecting the pride, or family.

CHEETAH

Catch her if you can! Cheetahs run faster than any other land animal. They sneak up on their prey, and then burst into action. They use their tail for balance as they chase. Their spines move easily for quick turns. But cheetahs are only good for short spurts of speed. They soon need a rest! They have two black "tear tracks" on either side of their nose, which help protect their eyes from the sun's glare. That's especially nice since, unlike most big cats, cheetahs hunt during the day, not at night.

In 2018, scientists spotted a super-rare black leopard. The last time one was seen was in 1909.

Cheetahs can run up to 70 mph (112 kph)—that's as fast as a speeding car on a freeway.

LEOPARD

African leopards are content almost anywhere. In the savanna, they hunt smaller game than lions do. They have the power to climb high trees, and they often drag an animal they've caught up there with them. This keeps their dinner safe from hungry hyenas waiting below.

CAMEL

These animals are known as the "ships of the desert." They have ways to protect themselves from their harsh, dry home. Two rows of very long eyelashes keep their eyes clear of blowing sand. So does a clear third lid on each eye. Camels can also shut their nostrils. And their humps store fat. When they're hungry or thirsty this fat feeds them. There are two camel species: bactrian, which have two humps, and dromedary, which have only one.
HOME TURF Bactrians live in China's Gobi Desert. Dromedaries live in North Africa and the Middle East.

While camels have been helping humans carry things across the desert for thousands of years, they like to spit on people!

HARSH LIFE IN THE DESERT

They can be the driest places on Earth and are usually burning hot during the day and freezing cold at night. It's a hard place to live, but these hardy creatures have found out how to survive.

Young hoopoes can run extremely fast, even before they can fly.

GREATER HOOPOE-LARK

This bird is a trickster. If an enemy comes near its nest, they go far away and pretend to be hurt. The predator comes after them and the hoopoe-lark suddenly flies off. The babies back home stay safe. On land, their long legs are a plus, because they keep their bodies safely above the hot desert ground.
HOME TURF Sahara Desert to the Middle East; India to Iran

SCORPION

Watch out for that tail! That's where the scorpion keeps its stinger, which it uses to kill its insect or lizard dinner—but it can be painful (occasionally even deadly) to humans as well. Scorpions hunt mostly at night. During the scorching daytime, they escape the heat by burrowing underground.
HOME TURF All deserts except the cold ones

Scorpions are related to spiders, ticks and mites. They all have eight legs, and belong to the group called arachnids.

DESERT TORTOISE

These tough reptiles burrow down to avoid the heat. They dig long tunnels and buddy up. Sometimes 20 tortoises might hide together from the blazing sun. They also dig narrow holes in the sand, then they wait for rain. A rain-filled hole means water to drink!

HOME TURF Deserts in the American Southwest and northwestern Mexico

A pet or captive tortoise should never be let loose. It won't know how to survive in the wild. If it can't be kept, contact an animal expert.

DESERT PUPFISH

These little swimmers can live in both fresh water and salt water. They can survive even in water temperatures as high as 108 F (42 C). And they eat mosquitoes—a plus for humans!

HOME TURF Death Valley in eastern California and other southwestern United States desert areas

ROADRUNNER

You may have seen this bird in cartoons zooming past its enemy, Wile E. Coyote. The roadrunner really does run like crazy—up to 26 mph (42 kph). Their long tail feathers give them balance as they speed after their prey, including small mammals and insects.

HOME TURF American Southwest and Mexico

Sunbaths are a treat after a cold night. They lift up their feathers so the sun shines on them.

PAINTED LADY BUTTERFLY

With their beautiful orange-and-black wings, these butterflies are well named. Like hundreds of other butterfly species, they reside in deserts, but they live everywhere else, too. Painted ladies live in more places than any other type of butterfly. Alas, these beauties only live for about two weeks.

HOME TURF Deserts and meadows everywhere but Antarctica

us & them

We use our tongues to taste and ears to hear. Butterflies taste with their feet and hear with their antennae!

During migration, painted lady butterflies can travel up to 100 miles (160 km) a day.

Most mom and dad jackals stay together for life. Very few other mammal species do this.

COMMON JACKAL

There are a few jackal species, but this one is a desert animal. They don't mind the heat. They hide in bushes during the day. At sunset, they join in a chorus of spooky cries. When it gets dark, the jackals go hunting for rodents, birds and reptiles.

HOME TURF Africa, Asia and eastern Europe

GILA MONSTER

A few lizards are venomous, and this desert-dwelling lizard is one of them! A gila (HEE-luh) monster's bite is painful but not deadly. They are slow-moving, lazy creatures. And like so many other desert animals, they hide underground from the heat during the day. A good meal is birds' eggs or baby mammals.
HOME TURF Mojave, Sonora and Chihuahua deserts of the southwestern United States and northwestern Mexico

Gila monsters don't strike with fangs. They chomp down hard with their teeth and don't let go. Sometimes you can pry them loose with a stick in the mouth.

These birds are sometimes also called chicken hawks.

Huge numbers of locusts are known as a plague.

RED-TAILED HAWK

This raptor likes a high perch. From above, it waits to spy some tasty prey—small mammals including rodents and rabbits. Then, watch out! Red-tails are known to dive-bomb, shooting straight down at high speed. They live in all kinds of places. But deserts give them the wide-open spaces they like best.
HOME TURF North and Central America

DESERT LOCUST

Can you say giant grasshopper? That's really all this big insect is, growing up to 3 inches (7.6 cm) long! The scary thing is when a giant group of them gets together and flies in massive clouds. They are big eaters too. A bunch of them could strip a whole field clean in minutes, and they've been known to destroy crops.
HOME TURF Central Africa, Arabian Peninsula and parts of Asia stretching to India

BILBY

This guy may look a bit like a long-nosed rabbit, but it's a marsupial. They have a pouch for carrying babies. The pouches open downward, so those little joeys can't peek out. But that's OK, because bilbies have terrible eyesight. They rely on keen hearing and smell to get around.
HOME TURF Northwestern Australia

The word "bilby" comes from Australia's native people. It means "long-nosed rat."

year of the locust

In the summer of 1874, an enormous swarm of Rocky Mountain locusts came across the U.S. plains—120 billion of them. They darkened the sun as they flew. When they landed, the locusts ate everything in sight—crops, trees and grassy fields. People starved. But many survived by eating locust bodies cooked in butter. Yum?

THAT'S FOXY!

Foxes can adjust to change better than a lot of species. So it's not surprising they are found in many different types of surroundings. More than 10 types of foxes live in deserts of the world. Meet some of these sly guys!

Fennec foxes pant *a lot* when the weather gets hot—up to 690 breaths per minute! This helps keep their body temperatures from getting too high.

TIBETAN SAND FOX

Compared to a fennec, this fox's ears look a bit shrunken. And people call it square-headed. Tibetan foxes live on very high, level ground that's dry and desertlike. They shy away from humans. But they love to eat pika (a small mammal).
HOME TURF India, Nepal, Bhutan and China

FENNEC FOX

The world's smallest fox, they are just around 14 inches (35.6 cm) tall and weigh about 2 pounds (0.9 kg). Their huge ears help them hear prey hiding in the sand and also help them cool off.
HOME TURF North Africa, throughout the Sahara Desert and east to Sinai and Arabia

Humans are the only known enemy of the sand fox. People hunt them for their fur.

KIT FOX

What's on the menu for a kit fox? Kangaroo rat! Well, that and other small mammals. But these hunters actually don't need to drink water, because their prey provides enough. Look sharp if you come across a patch of desert land filled with holes. These might be the work of a kit fox. These desert dwellers love to dig! And here's a funny thing: All baby foxes are called kits. So a baby kit fox would be a kit fox kit!

HOME TURF The American Southwest, and northern and central Mexico

in plain sight

Why are desert foxes mostly tan-colored? It's called camouflage (KA-muh-flaazh). Many animals are colored to blend in with their surroundings. This keeps them better hidden from something that might want to eat them! It also helps them sneak up on prey.

Blanford's foxes are known by lots of other names. Among them: dog fox, king fox, royal fox, black fox and cliff fox.

Like all foxes, kit foxes eat meat. But sometimes there's just not enough of that. In that case they've been known to chow down on fruit and cactus parts.

BLANFORD'S FOX

Only the fennec fox is smaller than this little cutie. Blanford's foxes have bodies that are about 16-20 inches (40-50 cm) long and weigh about 7-9 pounds (3-4 kg). Most desert foxes eat rodents and insects. Blanford's foxes like insects too—including locusts—but their diet also includes melons and seedless grapes. They are named for the English naturalist William Thomas Blanford, who first described them in 1877.

HOME TURF Southwest Asia, Israel and the Arabian Peninsula

CHAPTER 6
BRAVING ICE & SNOW

The top and bottom of our planet are like giant freezers. At the top there's the North Pole, also known as the Arctic. At the bottom is the South Pole, or Antarctica. These are very challenging places to live. Yet some animals not only survive but even thrive in the extreme cold.

Emperor penguins have lots of ways to survive in chilly Antarctica, from four layers of feathers to plenty of body fat.

COLD-LOVING CRITTERS

Here are some real ice-and-snow fans from the world's polar parts.

POLAR BEAR

Nothing says North Pole like the polar bear! Mother bears crawl into a den in the snow. There they give birth, always during winter. Polar bears are the only bear species that needs ice—they stand on a chunk and wait to catch a nice fat seal meal! Their black foot pads have bumps that help keep them from slipping. But the breaking up of polar ice is making it harder for these bears to survive.

Polar bears sometimes politely touch noses. Usually it means one bear is asking the other to share a fresh-caught meal.

Ribbon seals get around by slapping down their front flippers, one at a time.

RIBBON SEAL

This standout striped seal is hard to miss on a block of ice. Its "ribbons" develop over the first three years of its life. Ribbon seals need the sea ice as a landing space for giving birth. They also molt and raise their pups on the ice. Then it's time to slip back into the freezing water.

ARCTIC LAMPREY

This weird, eel-like fish has a mug only its mother could love! The lamprey has no jaws. But check out that mouth. It's just an open ring. Inside is a scary-looking set of little fangs. Lamprey grab their prey, clamp on and suck out their blood. Good thing that prey is other fish, not people!

Baby lampreys have no eyes or mouths. It takes between three and seven years to grow these parts!

The other species of minke whale is called the common minke. You can find these animals in all the oceans of the world.

ANTARCTIC MINKE WHALE

Minke (MINK-ee) whales are small, curious and fast swimmers. All minke whales are baleen whales. That means they have baleen—rows of thin, comblike teeth. To eat, baleen whales take huge gulps of water. The water is full of small prey called krill. The whales then push the water out through the baleen. But their food can't get out! This species lives in the icy waters of the Antarctic. In winter, some of them migrate to warmer waters, while others stay behind.

Walruses are social—they share food and like to hang out in packs.

WALRUS

Walrus lovers say these big marine mammals are friendly—unless you mess with their babies. They're also super smart. They prefer swimming in shallow waters. They use their whiskers to sense food in dark ocean waters. Walruses rely on their powerful tusks to help pull their huge bodies out of the water.

SNOWY OWL

This bird is a big fluff ball of thick feathers. Snowy owls use their sharp claws, or talons, to grab their prey from the ground. The males are all white. The females' white feathers are marked with bands of black.

Snowy owls have a wingspan of 4–5 feet (1–1.5 m).

myth & reality

Part of an old nursery rhyme goes, "A wise old owl lived in an oak. The more he saw the less he spoke." Where did the idea of "wise old owls" come from? Maybe from the ancient Greek people. The owl was holy to Athena, the Greek goddess of knowledge.

EMPEROR PENGUIN

"Emperor" is another word for king. And these birds are kings of the penguin world. They're bigger than all other penguins. The mother emperor lays one egg in the harsh cold. Then she takes off to the sea. The father tucks the egg onto his feet and covers it with a "brood patch." This is a bit of featherless skin topped by thick feathers—like a down jacket for the egg! He stands there for about two months. He doesn't even eat until the baby bird hatches.

Emperors are about 4 feet (120 cm) tall—about the same size as a 6-year-old kid!

ANTARCTIC ICEFISH

Icefish depend on extremely cold water, as low as 29 F (-1.8 C). All vertebrates, including humans, have red blood—except the icefish. These fish have milky-pale blood. Their hearts are white, too, not red like human hearts. In some icefish you can see the brain right inside its head!

NARWHAL

Talk about tusks! The narwhal's long spiral tusk sets it apart from most creatures. No wonder it's sometimes called the unicorn of the sea. The tusk is actually a super-sensitive tooth. This "big tooth" may have many uses. Male narwhals sometimes fight with their tusks—this is called "tusking."

Some narwhals never grow a tusk. Others grow two. Some narwhal tusks gradually get smaller over time.

Anemones are related to jellyfish. And like jellyfish, they sting with their tentacles.

Some of these birds have a blue ring around their eyes. Others have a purple or red ring.

ANTARCTIC SEA ANEMONE

They look like flowers. They're even named after one. But anemones (uh-NEH-muh-neez) are animals. They're found in all the world's oceans. A new one was found in Antarctic in 2010. It buries itself in solid underwater ice, and its tentacles stick out of the ice like little fingers.

TARDIGRADE

Deserts, mountains, volcanoes, oceans. Even Antarctica. Tardigrades (TAHR-duh-graydz) can survive pretty much anywhere. But they're so tiny you can't see them with your bare eyes. They can handle extremes of cold and heat. No wonder the clawed and crumpled-looking tardigrade is known as Earth's toughest creature.

BLUE-EYED SHAG

When tired sailors see this bird they breathe a sigh of relief: They know land is near, because blue-eyed shags never stray far from their nests to feed. They're the only bird in their habitat with a year-round nest. But their babies are born without feathers. That's cold!

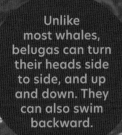

Unlike most whales, belugas can turn their heads side to side, and up and down. They can also swim backward.

Arctic lamprey
Beluga whale
Narwhal
Polar bear
Ribbon seal
Snowy owl
Walrus

Antarctic icefish
Antarctic minke whale
Antarctic sea anemone
Blue-eyed shag
Emperor penguin
Tardigrade

BELUGA WHALE

Belugas may look all white but they're dark gray at birth. The lump of fat on their foreheads is called a "melon." Belugas wiggle their melon to direct the sounds they make. In deep, dark ocean waters, whales can't see much, so belugas make a lot of strange sounds to communicate. They squeak, whistle, click, moan, groan and chirp.

WINTER WHITES

Many polar animals stay white year-round. But these
Arctic animals put on their white coats only when the snow is flying!

PTARMIGAN

Summer color: mostly all brown or speckled shades of brown, black and yellow. The ptarmigan's (TAHR-muh-gun's) winter feathers carry air bubbles. This makes them look dazzling white. Some ptarmigan species keep some black tail feathers in winter. But all grow white feather "booties" to walk more easily in the snow.

SNOWSHOE HARE

Summer color: brown or brownish-gray. When the days get shorter the hare starts the job of color-changing. It can take more than two months for a hare's fur to turn fully white.

PEARY CARIBOU

Summer color: from silvery-brown to a thicker, lighter-colored coat. Some, but not all, go completely white. "Caribou" and "reindeer" are two names for the same animal. Caribou are wild animals. Those that live with people are called reindeer. Only among caribou do females grow antlers.

COLLARED LEMMING

Summer color: gray, brown, reddish-brown and cream-color mixes; sometimes with dark stripes on their backs or faces. They are the only lemming species to go all white in the winter. These little rodents also grow sharp double claws in winter—all the better to scrape and dig through thick ice and snow.

eye-opener

Caribou have golden eyes in the summer. In winter their eyes turn blue. No other mammal's eyes change color with the weather.

TAKING TO THE SKY

Thousands of bird species have the superpower of flight. They glide, dip and soar. Some dive-bomb. Whatever their skills, birds bring magic to the world. Here's a bird's-eye view of a few cool feathered creatures!

A peregrine falcon can swoop down at up to 242 mph (389 kph)—almost five times faster than a car going the speed limit on a freeway!

MIGHTY FLYERS

Some birds stand out when it comes to staying power. That means they have the strength to dive, sail and go amazing distances—with ease.

An albatross can fly for eight hours without even flapping its wings once.

myth & reality

Some old myths say that killing an albatross is bad luck. And seeing one at sea is said to mean stormy weather is coming. These ideas probably spread from old poems and sailors' tales. At sea, these giant birds were a part of everyday life.

ALBATROSS

This big seabird can really go the distance! The albatross' wingspan is greater than any other bird's. Some measure 12 feet (3.6 m) from tip to tip (about as long as two average-size men lying head to head). That makes endless gliding a breeze. They can fly more than a year without landing. Albatross feathers do fine in water. It's just the sharks down there that scare them!

HOME TURF Mostly in the Southern Hemisphere

These are the only birds that fly straight into clouds on purpose. And it's a bumpy ride in there!

FRIGATE BIRD

These big, wide-winged birds can sail the skies nonstop for weeks. They can't rest on the water because their feathers aren't waterproof, so they just soar over the seas. When it's time to eat they go fishing—even while flying!

HOME TURF Worldwide near warm islands and coastlines near the equator

ARCTIC TERN

When seasons change, many birds migrate from chilly to warmer places. Later, they return home. The Arctic tern is a migration hero. It flies all the way from the Arctic to the bottom of the world, Antarctica. No other bird flies a longer distance—twice a year!—to reach its new home.

HOME TURF The Arctic and Antarctica

Peregrine vision is eight times better than ours. They can spot prey from a distance of about 15 city blocks away.

PEREGRINE FALCON

Peregrine (PEHR-uh-gruhn) falcons are raptors. They are also the largest of all hawks. That comes in handy when hunting. These birds like to lunch mostly on smaller birds. They catch their unlucky prey in midflight—diving from above, of course!

HOME TURF Everywhere around the world except Antarctica

BIG SHOWOFFS

Male birds are usually more brightly colored than females. And these flashy five could all win a bird beauty contest!

These birds are actually peafowl. The males are called peacocks; the females are called peahens and the babies are called peachicks.

PEACOCK

If you want attention, grow a tail like this one! This tail is called a train, and it takes three years to fully grow. Some peacock trains are as long as 6 feet (1.8 m). The peacock drags its train along the ground till it's ready to show off. Then he (only the males have a colorful train) raises it like a wide fan and really shakes a tail feather.
HOME TURF Central Africa, Southeast Asia, India

There are 42 different bird-of-paradise species, all beautiful and bizarre. The males have more colors than other bird-of-paradise species.

WILSON'S BIRD-OF-PARADISE

These rain forest birds may be small, but what other bird can brag of a curly tail like Wilson's bird-of-paradise? And its bright blue head isn't coming from feathers—it's a patch of bare skin. To attract a female, the male Wilson clears a patch of ground. Then he does a fancy dance. The female watches from above. If she doesn't dig his moves, she flies off.
HOME TURF New Guinea

The color of flamingo feathers comes from what they feed on. That's why different species have different colors.

1,200
Number of times a hummingbird's heart beats per minute.

A hummingbird can fly upside down and backward. But it can't hop or walk. Its feet are only for perching.

SWORD-BILLED HUMMINGBIRD
The swordbill's super-long bill is very useful. The bird plunges its bill deep inside tube-shaped flowers. Out comes a straw-like tongue, which means it's time to sip up the flower's nectar.
HOME TURF South America

GOULDIAN FINCH
Many finches are brightly colored. But the Gouldian (GOOL-dee-uhn) stands out with its day-glo colors. No wonder it's also known as the rainbow finch. Gouldian finches are social birds. Sometimes hundreds of them gather together in a giant flock.
HOME TURF Mostly northern Australia

CHILEAN FLAMINGO
The Chilean (chill-AY-uhn) flamingo struts its stuff along the coastlines. It wades in shallow lakes and near riverbanks. In group flights, they sometimes form a V-shape. They are related to the more whitish-colored greater flamingo.
HOME TURF South America

Most Gouldian finches have black faces. Some have red. Yellow faces are very rare. The black-faced ones are risk-takers.

BIRDS OF PREY

The word raptor comes from the Latin language. It means "to carry away." These are the bird world's fiercest hunters. They have hooked beaks and razor-sharp talons. Their hearing and eyesight are extreme.

Like owls, harpies have a facial disk, or a circle of feathers around their head. They lift these feathers to help hear things.

HARPY EAGLE

Harpy eagles are the most powerful raptors. They build tree nests so big a grownup could easily fit in one. Harpies aren't built for soaring. They twist and turn between one tree and the next. They're great at hunting big game like sloths and monkeys, and those talons really come in handy—they're longer than a grizzly bear's claws!

HOME TURF Central and South America

myth & reality

The harpy eagle gets its name from ancient Greek mythology. The harpies were monster creatures. They had a bird's body and a human face. There are many stories about Greek harpies. One says they had the power of the fastest winds.

ANDEAN CONDOR

No raptor has a larger wingspan than Andean condors. And it's easy to tell the males from the females. This isn't true of other condor species. But the male Andean condor is born with a comb on its face. And each comb is different, like fingerprints. Condors are vultures. They're soaring scavengers, always on the lookout for dead meat.

HOME TURF Andes mountains; western South America to western Argentina

The condor has a bald head. That helps it stay clean when it sticks its head into a dead animal's body!

term to know

A **scavenger** (SKA-vuhn-jr) is a bird that eats dead animal flesh and other rotting material.

Philippine eagles are the only raptors with pale, blue-gray eyes and a blue beak.

PHILIPPINE EAGLE

The lion's-mane head, feathers and pale eyes make the Philippine (FILL-uh-peen) eagle look extra intense. It's the biggest of all eagles in terms of length and wing surface. But it isn't very picky when it comes to dinner—it goes for whatever is easiest to catch.

HOME TURF Philippine forests

WATER WINGS

Many bird species live around water. Shorebirds nest near water, and spend as much time walking on solid ground as floating. But the birds here are real water babies. That means they spend their days mostly in the water!

Puffins are known for their big, bright-colored beaks. And they have feet to match.

PUFFIN

Puffins are not much into flying—they're known to crash-land. They'd rather float in cold water. They're good swimmers and fishing comes easy for them. When they gather in groups onshore, they chatter nonstop. But at sea, they don't make a sound.
HOME TURF Mostly Iceland

PACIFIC LOON

At dusk the loon settles on the water in a lonely, woodsy place and sounds a haunting wail. It's a deep diver and good fisherman. But its legs are placed so far back on its body it can barely walk.
HOME TURF Mostly northern Canada and the Pacific coast

To get airborne, big heavy loons start on the water. They rise up and run straight across the water's surface, flapping their wings wildly. To get enough power for liftoff, they must run about as far as half a football field.

BLUE-FOOTED BOOBY

Everybody do the booby dance! When these males get going they stomp, strut and bop. Seeing them, you might laugh. But the ladies love it. Still, getting around on land is a clumsy thing. So boobies prefer the water. They are powerful divers. And they'd rather fly than walk any day!
HOME TURF Galápagos Islands, Pacific coast from Southern California to Peru, western coasts of Central and South America

Their blue-colored feet come from the fish the boobies eat. Scientists say the bluer the feet, the healthier the bird. That's why the females go for the guy with the bluest tootsies.

Mute swans often mate for life and are a symbol of lasting love. These beauties are easy to spot with their orange bills and black forehead knots.

MUTE SWAN

Mute swans were once found only in Europe. Now many glide around American waters too. But they can cause trouble. They're sometimes mean and they eat and destroy plants other animals need for food.
HOME TURF Northeast and Midwest U.S., British Isles, north-central Europe and Asia

STAYING GROUNDED

Some birds are stuck on Earth. They may be able to hop or jump or run like the wind, but flightless birds—like the ones here—will never take to the skies.

Rheas have longer wings than most flightless birds. Their main purpose is for balance when they're running.

GREATER RHEA

Many female rheas often lay eggs in the same nest. Then the father sits on them till they hatch. He watches over the new baby birds. He defends them like a madman. He'll even attack their mothers if they get too close!
HOME TURF Argentina, Bolivia, Uruguay, Paraguay and Brazil

GALÁPAGOS CORMORANT

The Galápagos is the only cormorant that can't fly. Their wings barely exist and their feathers aren't totally waterproof. But they have strong legs and webbed feet well-made for swimming. To hunt, they tuck in those wings, dive deep and spear a fish or an octopus.

HOME TURF
Galápagos Islands

They're not born with those jewel-colored eyes. The hue takes a while to appear.

These colorful-headed birds also lay colorful eggs that are bright green and giant-size!

KIWI

Not all flightless birds are big. The chicken-sized kiwi is related to bigger flightless birds though, including the ostrich, cassowary and emu. Kiwis have a sharp sense of smell. That's a good thing, because they don't see so well in the dark—and nighttime is their time to search for food.

HOME TURF Forests of New Zealand

Kiwis have whiskers and nostrils at the end of their beaks. And they can sneeze on purpose!

CASSOWARY

Meet the most dangerous bird in the world. Their middle toes have long, slice-and-dice claws which are deadly weapons. They'll charge an enemy at high speed and will head-butt, leap, peck and throw high-powered kicks. But when left alone, cassowaries are usually shy.

HOME TURF Australia and Southeast Asia

CHAPTER 8

INTO THE MYSTERIOUS DEEP

Earth's waters are home to countless animals—maybe a million species or more. Only a small part of our huge oceans has been explored. But on these pages are some amazing species that have been found!

The Earth has almost three times as much water as land. And nearly all that water is in the world's oceans.

DIVING BELL SPIDER

This odd little spider lives its whole life underwater. So how does it get air? Easy! First it builds a little "bubble nest," called a diving bell. The spider attaches the diving bell to an underwater plant. Inside the bell is a water-free space filled with air. That's a good, dry place to raise babies!

HOME TURF Lakes and ponds in Siberia, central Asia, northern and central Europe, and some parts of Japan

Diving bell spiders hibernate from November until February in a strong, airtight bell.

FRESHWATER FREAKS

If you've ever swum in an ocean, you've been in salt water. But rivers, lakes and streams contain fresh water. Compared to the oceans, there's very little fresh water on Earth, but these bodies of water are still full of life. That includes some very unusual animals—like these!

OLM

These very rare pinkish salamanders aren't easy to find. They spend their lives in the deepest and darkest caves. No wonder they're nearly blind. Some live longer than 100 years—all in the water!
HOME TURF Caves in parts of Italy and the western Balkans

PIRANHA

This fish has a bad rap—with good reason! The piranha (puh-RAH-nah) is a vicious hunter and killer. They often hunt in packs, called shoals. To be fair, some piranhas are plant-eaters. But the meat-eaters use their needle-sharp teeth to go for their enemy's eyes or tail. They're attracted to splashing, and to blood in the water. So watch out!
HOME TURF The Amazon Basin in South America

There are three kinds of salamander: those that live in water, those that live on land and those that live both on land and in water.

myth & reality

The Bella River goes through Romania, in central Europe. In the 1600s, the river flooded. With the flood came a surprise: Many strange, pale little creatures washed onto land. Villagers thought they were baby dragons. Scientists today think those "dragons" were olms swept out of their caves.

Piranhas can smell a single drop of blood in water. How much water? Enough to fill more than a big bathtub.

OCEAN DWELLERS

Sea life remains mostly a mystery to humans, and new ocean species are being found all the time. The ones here have been known for ages. You might say they're like old friends!

The suckers on an octopus' arms work like taste buds. And if they lose an arm, a new one grows in its place.

OCTOPUS

Octopuses are very smart. They can find their way through mazes. They can twist off a jar lid with any one of their eight arms. Octopuses like underwater hideouts such as caves and empty shells. They have no bones, so they can slither into cracks between rocks—most can squeeze into even the tiniest openings!

HOME TURF All oceans of the world

GIANT CLAM

Giant is right! This animal sits on the seabed looking big and beautiful. It lives in coral reefs. Some are as wide as 4 feet (1.2 m). A single giant clam may weigh about the same as two newborn elephants! Healthy clams are brightly colored. Each one has a different color pattern than all others. When they're dead or dying, they turn white.

HOME TURF Coral reefs in the Indian Ocean, the South Pacific and around some parts of South Africa

A giant clam can make a pearl. The largest one ever weighed nearly 75 pounds (34 kg) and was worth $100 million!

myth & reality

Old tales warned divers that giant clams could grab a person swimming by. But their shells close so slowly they could never trap anyone!

CORAL

Surprise! This is neither plant nor rock. Coral are living animals, and there are about 6,000 species of them. They're a huge, important part of sea life. Coral reefs are like big apartment buildings for millions of other species. Some of these include seahorses, sea turtles and sponges (which are also animals!). Some coral reefs are hundreds of years old. But the world's coral is dying at a troubling rate. This is mainly because of human activities such as overfishing and water pollution.

HOME TURF Oceans worldwide; reef-building corals are only in warm, shallow waters near the equator

1 out of 4

Number of ocean species that need coral to stay alive —they find food and shelter inside the reef.

The world's largest coral reef is the Great Barrier Reef. It lies east of Australia. It's so big you can see it from space.

SEAHORSE

The seahorse is a very different kind of fish. The dads and moms usually mate for life. Each morning the pair meets up. They change colors as they get closer. They move around in a little "dance." When it's time to have babies, Dad does all the work. He carries the eggs in a special pouch on his body. About two to four weeks later he gives birth!

HOME TURF Warm waters throughout the world

A seahorse has no stomach. It takes in food through its snout, or nose.

save the seahorses!

Every year, about 1 million seahorses are caught for people's aquariums. But these seahorses only live a few weeks. If this doesn't stop, the world will have no more of these magical creatures.

LION'S MANE JELLYFISH

The lion's mane is the biggest of all jellyfish. That "mane" is a mass of hanging tentacles. Some lion's mane jellies have as many as 1,200 of them! But beware: They come with a powerful sting.

HOME TURF Arctic and North Pacific Ocean from Alaska to Washington

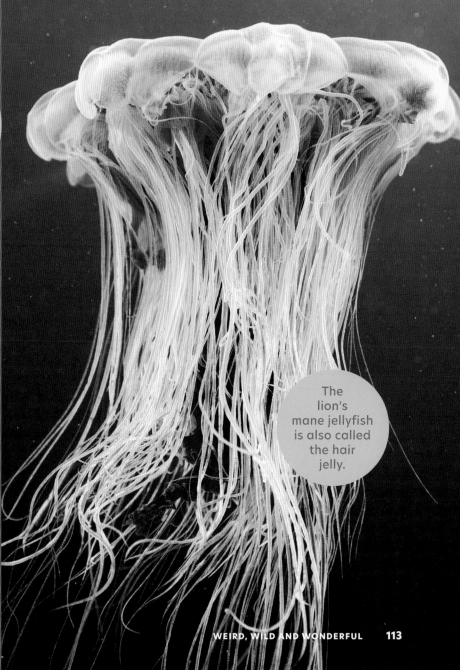

The lion's mane jellyfish is also called the hair jelly.

CREEPIES OF THE DEEP

A lot of deep-sea animals may be lovely to look at, but these creatures are straight out of nightmares and horror movies!

TASSELLED WOBBEGONG

Its looks are as strange as its name. The wobbegong (WAH-bee-gung) is a carpet shark. The front of its head has fringes, or tassels. It lies on the ocean bottom, hiding in plain sight! You wouldn't even know it's a living thing. A small fish swims by and the sly wobbegong's mouth snaps open. It sucks in its meal!

HOME TURF Great Barrier Reef; waters of the western Pacific, including New Guinea, eastern Indonesia and northern Australia

"Wobbegong" comes from an Indigenous Australian language. It means "shaggy beard."

BLOBFISH

Blobfish are a little low on good looks. But it's not their fault. Blobfish have no skeletons, so they look pretty saggy out of the deep water. Down in the sunless depths, though, the water presses hard on their bodies and they look more like "normal" fish!
HOME TURF Mariana Trench and off the coasts of Australia, Tasmania and New Zealand

The blobfish lives in very deep waters, so very little is known about it.

what is the mariana trench?

Almost 7 miles (11 km) below the surface of the water in the South Pacific, the Mariana Trench is the deepest place on Earth. It's more than 1,500 miles (2,414 km) long and about 43 miles (69 km) wide on average.

RED-LIPPED BATFISH

Hello, Hollywood! This fish might look like it's wearing a lot of ruby-red lipstick on those lips, but they're straight from nature. So are the red-lipped batfish's fins, which kind of look like legs (they even move like legs). Of course this fish can swim. But why bother? Strolling the sandy ocean floor is even better.
HOME TURF Waters near the Galápagos Islands

Scientists don't know what these flashy lips are for—maybe they help the fish get an underwater date!

A hatchet is a thin, sharp ax used for cutting. So this fish's name is not surprising. Its body is very thin and shaped like a hatchet blade.

DEEP-SEA HATCHETFISH

Some hatchetfish live in fresh water. But this one is a deep-ocean species. It has little pale-blue lights that run in rows along its underside. At night it swims up to more shallow waters to look for food. When the sun comes up, it's back to the blackout world.

HOME TURF Mariana Trench and most warm ocean waters around the world

on the menu

These sea creatures sound good enough to eat, right? But think again!

SEA CUCUMBER

Some people really do eat these things. They can be pickled, fried or eaten raw. They're supposed to be good for you. But they're slimy and tasteless. Yuck!

FRIED EGG JELLYFISH

This isn't your everyday breakfast food. For starters, this jellyfish is venomous. But it's not very harmful to humans.

ICE CREAM CONE WORM

That cone looks pretty. But you wouldn't want to eat it. It's all sand! And the worm's innards are soft and squishy.

FANFIN SEA DEVIL

The fanfin's mouth is too terrifying for words! All sea devils are part of a group called anglerfish. Sticking out from this fish's snout is the "angler," which lights up in the dark. The fanfin's so-called fin-rays also carry tiny lights. This "light show" attracts prey. The fanfin's relative, the black sea devil, uses the same trick. And it's just as hideous to look at! Scientists think the fanfin's fin-rays may help them feel the world around them, like a cat's whiskers do.

HOME TURF Mariana Trench and all oceans

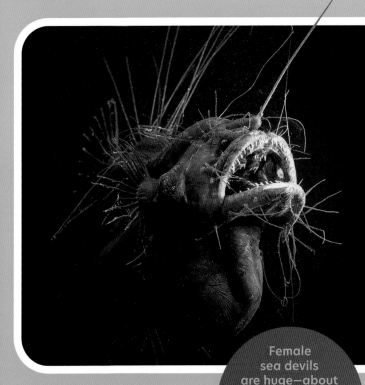

48
jet planes

About the amount of water pressure you would feel stacked on top of you in the deepest point of the ocean—enough to dissolve your bones!

Female sea devils are huge—about 8 inches (20 cm)—compared to the tiny males, which are only 0.5 inches (1.3 cm).

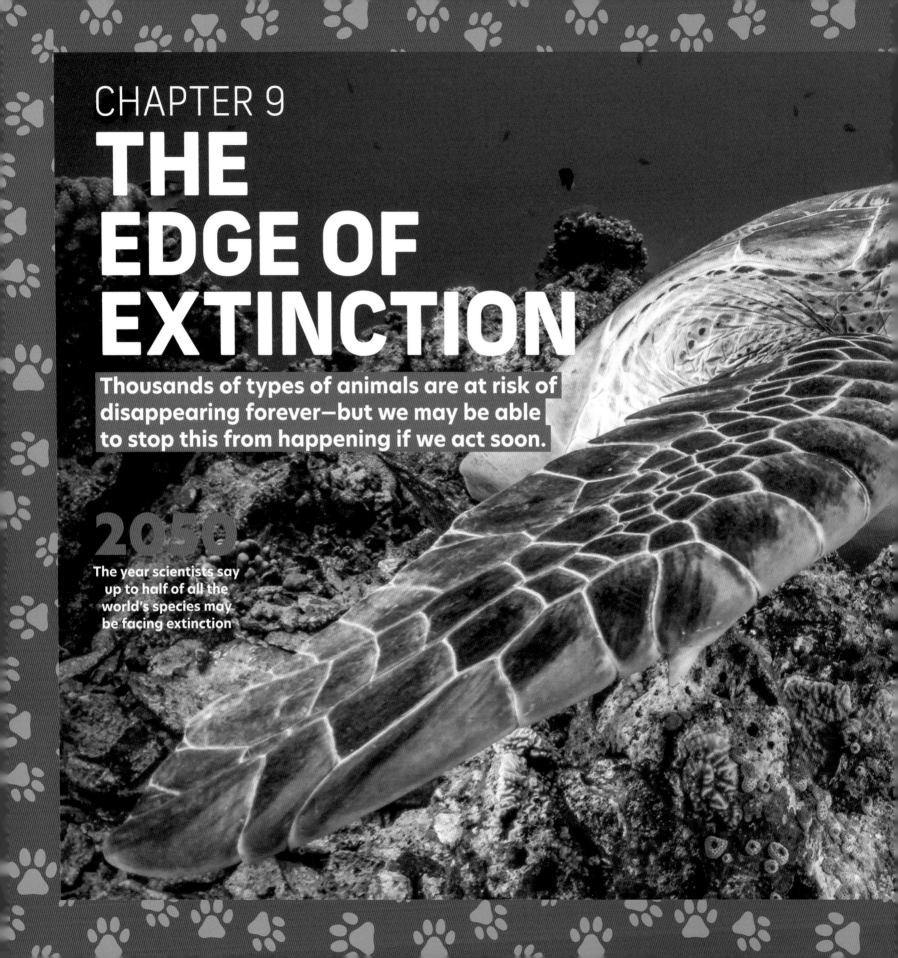

CHAPTER 9

THE EDGE OF EXTINCTION

Thousands of types of animals are at risk of disappearing forever—but we may be able to stop this from happening if we act soon.

2050

The year scientists say up to half of all the world's species may be facing extinction

It's hard to imagine Earth without its millions of amazing creatures. Sure, all kinds of species no longer exist. Take dinosaurs, for example. Over time, some species die out and new ones show up. That's just the way nature works. And usually these changes happen pretty slowly.

But today, these kinds of changes are taking place way too fast. Thousands of species may soon be lost forever. Nearly every animal in this book is at risk to some degree. This is not nature at work. It's the human species. People's actions are causing most of the troubles wild animals face.

Exactly how many animals are on the edge of extinction? It's hard to say. Different scientists give different numbers. The animals most in danger of extinction are called critically endangered. The list of which animals are the most critically endangered varies, too.

But while the numbers and lists change, one thing won't be altered. Every living thing on this planet is connected—humans, other animals and plants. When some species are gone it affects all the others, often in harmful ways. So the animals at risk need our help— and fast! Many people, called conservationists (kahn-sur-VAY-shun-ists), are working to save them. Maybe you'll find ways to help too.

12 AMAZING ANIMALS IN BIG TROUBLE

There are so many more endangered animals than these! But there are only a few left of most of the ones listed here.

HAWKSBILL SEA TURTLE They use their narrow beaks to eat sponges from reefs.

GIANT IBIS It's the national bird of Cambodia, and there are only about 300 left.

AMUR LEOPARD This beautiful beast from the far east of Russia is hunted for its spotted fur. Only about 70 are left in the wild.

TAPANULI ORANGUTAN The world's rarest great ape (only about 700 remain in Indonesia) was just discovered in 1997.

CEYLON ROSE BUTTERFLY This graceful insect is threatened by habitat loss in Sri Lanka.

SUMATRAN RHINOCEROS There are very few of these Asian rhinos left in the wild. The babies are tiny and woolly.

SAOLA (SOW-lah) This extremely rare animal, found only at the Vietnam/Laos border, is also called the Asian unicorn.

GHARIAL The croc with a funny-looking snout has only two places left to call home.

ARCHEY'S FROG Masters of camouflage, they are among the world's oldest frogs.

KAKAPO New Zealand's flightless "owl parrot" is the heaviest parrot in the world.

AXOLOTL This small amphibian is found only around Xochimilco, Mexico.

NORTH ATLANTIC RIGHT WHALE This is the most endangered large whale—less than 400 are estimated to remain.

the human problem

Why are so many animals in danger of extinction? Here are some of the biggest reasons today.

DESTRUCTION OF ANIMAL HABITATS We clear forests and other land for logging, farming and homes; and build projects that destroy habitats, such as dams and pipelines.

HUNTING AND POACHING Some people illegally kill or take animals or parts of animals for sale or use in products.

WATER AND SOIL POLLUTION Industries may dump chemicals into water and soil. We also throw tons of plastic into the oceans and use fishing nets that trap sea animals.

DISEASE AND PREDATORS Humans can introduce illnesses that can make other animals sick, or we bring in animals that outnumber and hunt down those species that already live there.

how to help

Check these websites. You'll learn a lot about endangered animals. You might also discover what needs to be done to help them stay alive.

DOSOMETHING.ORG A movement of young people all around the world helping the planet.

EARTHRANGERS.ORG Become an earth ranger and learn how to help!

DEFENDERS.ORG/WILDLIFE Learn more about many endangered animals and get an adoption kit.

CENTENNIAL BOOKS

An Imprint of
Centennial Media, LLC
1111 Brickell Avenue, 10th Floor
Miami, FL 33131, U.S.A.

CENTENNIAL BOOKS is a trademark of Centennial Media, LLC

ISBN 978-1-951274-86-3

Distributed by
Simon & Schuster, Inc.
1230 Avenue of the Americas
New York, NY 10020, U.S.A.

For information about custom editions, special sales and premium and corporate purchases,
please contact Centennial Media at contact@centennialmedia.com.

Manufactured in China

10 9 8 7 6 5 4 3 2 1

Publishers & Co-Founders Ben Harris, Sebastian Raatz
Editorial Director Annabel Vered
Creative Director Jessica Power
Executive Editor Janet Giovanelli
Features Editor Alyssa Shaffer
Writer Pamela Dell
Deputy Editors Ron Kelly, Anne Marie O'Connor
Managing Editor Lisa Chambers
Design Director Martin Elfers
Senior Art Director Pino Impastato
Art Directors Patrick Crowley, Jaclyn Loney, Natali Suasnavas, Joseph Ulatowski
Copy/Production Patty Carroll, Angela Taormina
Senior Photo Editor Jenny Veiga
Photo Editor Antoinette Campana
Production Manager Paul Rodina
Production Assistant Alyssa Swiderski
Editorial Assistant Tiana Schippa
Sales & Marketing Jeremy Nurnberg